best
easy
day hikes
Olympics

Erik Molvar

FALCON™

HELENA, MONTANA

AFALCONGUIDE®

Falcon® Publishing is continually expanding its list of recreational guidebooks. All books include detailed descriptions, accurate maps, and all the information necessary for enjoyable trips. You can order extra copies of this book and get information and prices for other Falcon guidebooks by writing Falcon, P.O. Box 1718, Helena, MT 59624 or calling 1-800-582-2665. Also, please ask for a free copy of our current catalog. Visit our web site at http:\\www.falconguide.com

©1998 by Falcon® Publishing Co., Inc. Helena, Montana.

10 9 8 7 6 5 4 3 2 1

Falcon and FalconGuide are registered trademarks of Falcon Publishing Co., Inc.

Printed in Canada.

Cover photo by Joanne Lotter/Tom Stack & Associates.

Library of Congress Cataloging-in-Publication Data

Molvar, Erik.
    Best easy day hikes, Olympics / by Erik Molvar.
        p.   cm.
    ISBN 1-56044-606-4 (pbk.)
    1. Hiking—Washington (State)—Olympic Mountains—Guidebooks.
    2. Trails—Washington (State)—Olympic Mountains—Guidebooks.
    3. Olympic Mountains (Wash.)—Guidebooks.   I. Title.
    GV199.42W220486 1998
    917.97'940443—dc21   97-50009
                                                                          CIP

CAUTION

Outdoor recreational activities are by their very nature potentially hazardous. All participants in such activities must assume the responsibility for their own actions and safety. The information contained in this guidebook cannot replace sound judgment and good decision-making skills, which helps reduce the risk of exposure, nor does the scope of this book allow for disclosure of all the potential hazards and risks involved in such activities. Learn as much as possible about the outdoor recreational activities in which you participate, prepare for the unexpected, and be cautious. The reward will be a safer and more enjoyable experience.

♻ Text pages reprinted on recycled paper.

Contents

Acknowledgments

Thanks to Bill Baccus and Ruth Scott for providing information and reviewing this book. The introductory material is largely the work of Bill Schneider. Special thanks to my fiancée, Melanie Davidson, for providing good company during the field research.

Legend

Interstate	(00)	Picnic Area	⊤⊤
U.S. Highway	(00) (000)	Campground	▲
State or County Road	(00) (000)	Bridge	⊰⊱
Interstate Highway	⟹	Mine Site	✕
Paved Road	⟹	Cave	⊱
Unpaved Road, Graded	⟹	Cabins/Buildings	■
Unpaved Road, Poor	=====⟹	Ruins	◪
Trailhead	○	Ranger Station	🛈
Main Trail	~⌣⌣⌣	Elevation	X 9,782 ft.
Secondary Trail	~⌣~~		
Trailless Route	··········	Falls, Pouroff	⌣∥
River/Creek, Perennial	⌢⌣	Pass/Saddle	)(
Drainage, Intermittent Creek	⌢·⌣	Gate	▬
Spring	⌀		
		Map Orientation	N ⬆
Forest/Wilderness/ Park Boundary	⌐_⌐⌐‾⌐	Scale	

Scale

0   30   60

Miles

Introduction

What's a "best easy" hike?

Our national parks and forests serve as windows to the natural world, reservoirs of natural beauty and grandeur, and wellsprings of inspiration. As such, they are magnets to people who seek to re-establish their ties with nature, learn more about the world in which we live, or simply find a quiet escape from the hustle and bustle of modern society. Olympic National Park features mountain fastnesses clad in glaciers, mysterious rainforests, and a wild and rugged coastline, inviting the visitor to step into the natural world.

Anyone who travels widely in these areas will soon notice that there are two distinct categories of visitors—those who want to immerse themselves in the wilderness of Olympic National Park for several days at a time, and those who only have a day or two and would like a choice sampling of the special features of the area. This book is for the second group.

The materials for this guide were gathered as I researched the much larger and more comprehensive book, *Hiking Olympic National Park*. That larger book covers every trail in the park and the surrounding areas, and every coastal hiking route, including those which are neither best nor easy. *Best Easy Day Hikes Olympics* includes only short, less strenuous hikes that showcase the best features of the Olympic Peninsula.

These hikes vary in length, but most are short (less than 5 miles). Most lack big hills, and those few long grades that appear in this book are tackled in a leisurely fashion. All hikes are on easy-to-follow trails and beaches with no route-finding challenges. Trailhead access is easy for all hikes, and you can reach any of these trailheads with a low-clearance passenger car.

Some of the hikes in this book might not seem easy to some but will be easy to others. To help you decide, I've ranked the hikes from easiest to hardest. Please keep in mind that long does not always equal difficult. Other factors, such as elevation gain and trail conditions, have to be considered.

I hope you thoroughly enjoy your "best easy" hiking through the natural wonders of Olympic National Park.

—Erik Molvar

Ranking The Hikes

The following list ranks the hikes in this book from easiest to hardest.

Easiest
Madison Creek Falls
Sol Duc Falls
Maple Groves Nature Trail
Sam's River Loop
Ranger Hole
Spruce Nature Trail
Hoh River
Lover's Lane
Hall of Mosses Nature Trail
Hole-in-the-Wall Rock
Hurricane Ridge Loop
The Spruce Railroad Trail
Staircase Rapids
Hurricane Hill
Marymere Falls
Irely Lake
Ruby Beach
The Quillayute Needles
Cape Alava
Sand Point
Olympic Hot Springs
Heart o' the Forest Trail
West Fork Dosewallips Gorge
The South Fork of the Hoh
Lillian Ridge
Geyser Valley Loop
Mount Angeles
Elk Mountain
Hardest Mount Zion

Leave No Trace

Traveling in a national park such as Olympic is like visiting a famous museum. You obviously don't want to leave your mark on an art treasure in the museum. If everybody who visited the museum left one tiny mark, the piece of art would be destroyed—and what would a big building full of trashed art be worth? The same goes for pristine wilderness like that found in Olympic National Park. If we all left just one little mark on the landscape, the wilderness would soon be despoiled.

A wilderness can accommodate plenty of human use as long as everybody treats it with respect. But a few thoughtless or uninformed visitors can ruin it for everyone who follows. And the need for good manners applies to all wilderness visitors, not just backpackers. Day hikers should also adhere strictly to the "leave no trace" principles. The book *Leave No Trace* is a valuable resource for learning more about these principles (ordering information in back of this book).

Three Falcon Principles of Leave No Trace

- *Leave with everything you brought in.*
- *Leave no sign of your visit*
- *Leave the landscape as you found it.*

Most of us know better than to litter—in or out of the wilderness. Even the tiniest scrap of paper left along the trail or at the campsite detracts from the pristine character of the Olympic landscape. This means that you should pack out everything, even biodegradable items such as orange peels, which can take years to decompose. It's also a good idea to pick up any trash that less considerate hikers have left behind.

To avoid damaging the trailside soil and plants, stay on the main path. Avoid cutting switchbacks and venturing onto fragile vegetation. When hiking on trailless beaches, stick to unvegetated surfaces below the storm tide mark, and don't disturb the fragile animals in tide pools. When taking a rest stop, select a durable surface like a bare log, a rock, or a sandy beach.

Don't pick up "souvenirs," such as rocks, antlers, feathers, or wildflowers. The next person wants to discover them, too, and taking such souvenirs violates park regulations.

Avoid making loud noises that disturb the silence that others may be enjoying. Remember, sound travels easily in the outdoors. Be courteous.

When nature calls, use established outhouse facilities whenever possible. If these are unavailable, bury human waste 6 to 8 inches deep and pack out used toilet paper. This is a good reason to carry a lightweight trowel. Keep wastes at least 300 feet away from any surface water or boggy spots.

Finally, and perhaps most importantly, strictly follow the pack-it-in/pack-it-out rule. If you carry something into the wilderness, consume it completely or carry it out with you.

Leave no trace—put your ear to the ground in the wilderness and listen carefully. Thousands of people coming behind you are thanking you for your courtesy and good sense.

The Leeward Olympics

OVERVIEW

This region of the park lies on the leeward side of the Olympic Mountains. Prevailing winds from the southwest are pushed upward because of the mountains, and the air dumps its moisture on the western slopes as it cools. Little moisture remains for the northeastern corner of the range, which is known as a "rainshadow" area. The geology and ecology of the rainshadow is defined in many ways by this lack of precipitation. Glaciers that buried the central mountains during the last Ice Age filled only the valleys here, and the rounded ridgetops became refuges for alpine plants and animals amid a sea of glacial ice. An astonishing diversity of wildflowers can be found here to this day, occupying habitats that range from alpine tundra to semi-desert.

Farther south, an abundance of short rivers penetrates the rugged outer ranges of the Olympic Mountains on their way to Hood Canal. These rivers offer travel corridors into the interior of the park, where a high alpine country of rugged, glacier-clad peaks is interspersed with lush meadows filled with wildflowers. The climate here is a transition between the temperate rainforest of the west and the rainshadow forests of the northeast. Valley bottoms harbor a lush growth of vegetation, while the nearby slopes may have dry montane forests. Lake Cushman, which lies outside the park on private lands, is a prime attraction of the area. Its close proximity to Seattle translates into weekend crowds when the weather is sunny.

The Leeward Olympics

The interior of the region falls within Olympic National Park, while the outer ranges and foothills are managed by the Forest Service. There is a Forest Service visitor center in Quilcene, and a joint National Park Service–Forest Service ranger station is located at Hoodsport. Smaller Park Service ranger stations are staffed during the summer at Staircase and on the Dosewallips River.

There are Forest Service campgrounds on the Dosewallips, Duckabush, and Hamma Hamma rivers, and also at Big Creek and Lilliwaup Creek. In Olympic National Park there are campgrounds at Staircase and on the Dosewallips River, while the state of Washington maintains heavily developed campgrounds at Dosewallips and Lake Cushman state parks. Some services and facilities can be found along U.S. Highway 101 in the villages of Hoodsport, Eldon, and Brinnon. A wider array of services can be found at Quilcene.

1
STAIRCASE RAPIDS

Type of hike: Loop.
Total distance: 2 miles.
Elevation change: 200 foot gain, 200 foot loss.
Time required: 1 to 2 hours.
Maps: Mount Steel USGS; Custom Correct *Mount Skokomish–Lake Cushman*.
Finding the trailhead: From Hoodsport, drive west on Lake Cushman Road past Lake Cushman State Park. Turn left on Forest Road 24 and drive 6.6 miles to the Staircase Ranger Station. The hike begins at the Staircase Rapids Trailhead, across the auto bridge from the ranger station. The hike ends at the North Fork Skokomish Trailhead, up a paved street from the ranger station.

Key points:

0.0 Staircase Rapids Trailhead, south bank of North Fork Skokomish River.

0.2 Spur trail runs north to large western red cedar.

0.6 Spur trail to "Red Reef Pool."

0.7 Spur trail to "Dolly Varden Pool."

0.8 Junction with trail to Four Stream. Turn right to complete loop.

0.9 Trail crosses Rapids Bridge over the North Fork of the Skokomish River.

1.0 Junction with North Fork Skokomish Trail. Turn right.

1.5 Trail crosses the dry bed of Slate Creek.
1.9 Overlook above the North Fork of the Skokomish.
2.0 Hike ends at North Fork Skokomish Trailhead above Staircase Ranger Station.

The hike: A popular footpath follows the south bank of the Skokomish River's North Fork, passing foaming whitewater and deep pools on the river. A footbridge spans the river at mile 1, linking it to the North Fork Skokomish Trail for a pleasant loop trip. This is a great hike for folks who wish to

Staircase Rapids

view old-growth trees as well as the crystalline pools and rushing rapids on one of the major rivers of the Olympic Peninsula.

The hike begins near the Staircase Ranger Station, just across the bridge at the edge of an open meadow. The well-beaten trail parallels the river as it moves upward through the conifers and vine maples. Early in the hike, a spur path accesses a western redcedar that is more than 14 feet in diameter. The main trail wanders toward the riverbank, making periodic visits to the rapids for pleasant views of the rushing water and crystalline pools. After 0.6 mile, a spur path accesses a hole known locally as "Red Reef Pool." Here, the river has cut a channel through a shelf of limestone that is tinted red with oxidized iron. The water plunges over the shelf, then roils in the aquamarine depths of the pool. A little farther on, a second spur descends to "Dolly Varden Pool," its depths punctuated by enormous boulders.

The main trail continues upstream beside Staircase Rapids to reach a footbridge. The trail upriver to Four Stream has been abandoned farther upstream; cross the bridge to return to Staircase Ranger Station via the North Fork Skokomish Trail, an old road grade that is now a broad hiking avenue through the enormous old-growth timber. Take a short side trip upstream at this junction to visit a pure stand of bigleaf maple. To return to the starting point, follow the North Fork Skokomish Trail downstream as it passes through a lush lowland forest unrivaled in its richness and diversity. Ancient Douglas-fir, redcedar, and western hemlock tower above the path, and moss-draped vine and bigleaf maples thrive amid the conifers.

After 0.5 mile, a log footbridge leads across the dry channel of Slate Creek. The slopes above were denuded during the Beaver Fire of 1985, which was started by an illegal campfire. This stream and others like it experienced heavy flooding in the wake of the blaze, and massive quantities of gravel were washed down from the slopes. Near the end of the trek, the old road grade climbs to an open overlook above the river for farewell views of the water. The trail emerges in a parking lot above the Staircase Ranger Station.

2
RANGER HOLE

Type of hike: Out-and-back.
Total distance: 1.7 miles.
Elevation change: Minimal.
Time required: 45 minutes to 1.5 hours
Maps: USGS Mount Jupiter; Custom Correct *The Brothers–Mount Anderson*.
Finding the trailhead: From Brinnon, drive north on U.S. Highway 101 to milepost 310. Turn west on Duckabush Road (Forest Road 2510) and drive 3.9 miles to the marked trailhead.

The hike: The trail begins at the historic Interrorem Ranger Station. This tightly built log cabin with its distinctive pyramidal roof served as the original ranger headquarters for Mount Olympus National Monument, which was to become a national park in 1938. A self-guided nature trail of 0.2 mile loops through the forest behind the cabin, which has grown in the wake of logging that dates from the mid-1800s. Walk the interpretive trail as a prelude and you will be able to identify the plants of the lowland forest community.

The Ranger Hole Trail begins by winding southwest through a second-growth forest. It passes a modern clearcut before dropping sharply to reach the banks of the Duckabush River after 0.8 mile. Here, the river charts a foaming passage through a narrow slot in the bedrock, then spreads out into the placid and crystalline depths of Ranger Hole. Steelhead could once be seen holding in the depths of this pool during their spawning migrations. Siltation from clearcutting has since buried their spawning gravels in muck, and the adult steelhead population has been depleted by heavy fishing pressure.

Turn around here to complete the hike.

Ranger Hole

3
WEST FORK DOSEWALLIPS GORGE

Type of hike: Out-and-back.
Total distance: 4.8 miles.
Elevation change: 530-foot gain.
Time required: 2.5 to 4 hours.
Maps: USGS The Brothers; Custom Correct *The Brothers–Mount Anderson*.
Finding the trailhead: From mile 306.1 on U.S. Highway 101 in the north part of Brinnon, turn west on the Dosewallips Road (Forest Road 2610). Drive 15.5 miles to the trailhead at road's end.

Key points:
0.0   Trailhead.
0.1   First junction with Dosewallips Terrace Trail. Stay right.
0.5   Second junction with Dosewallips Terrace Trail. Stay right.
1.4   Junction with Anderson Pass Trail. Turn left.
1.6   Dose Forks Camp. Trail crosses Dosewallips River.
2.4   Bridge spans the chasm of the West Fork of the Dosewallips.

The hike: This hike visits the forested lowlands of the

Dosewallips River (pronounced doh-see-WAH-lups). This river is fed by melting glaciers, and the fine silt ground up by the glaciers has turned the water a translucent turquoise color. In addition to views of the water at Dose Forks Camp and the deep canyon of the West Fork, visitors will enjoy the silent grandeur of a climax coniferous forest.

Begin the trek by climbing the hillside beyond the Dosewallips Ranger Station. The Dose Terrace Trail soon loops away to the left, running along the riverbank only to return to the main trail 0.4 mile farther on. Meanwhile the Dosewallips trail climbs through a mature forest of tall, slender hemlock and Douglas-fir. After crossing Pass Creek, the climbing eases, and the surrounding ridges can be seen through gaps in the thinning canopy. The trail crosses a second woodland stream before reaching a major junction. After 1.4 miles the trail reaches a major fork, the West Fork Trail that runs to Dose Forks camping area and on to Anderson Pass drops down to the left, while the Dosewallips Trail ascends to the right.

Turn left onto the West Fork Trail, which immediately descends to the Dose Forks Camp. The tent sites are set amid a grove of immense Douglas-fir beside the swirling turquoise waters of the Dosewallips. Just beyond the camp is a sturdy bridge to the south bank of the river. Once there, the trail ascends briskly onto forested slopes high above the water.

The actual "forks" of the Dosewallips lie 0.6 mile above the camp, and the trail skirts to the edge of a steep bluff to overlook the converging waters of the west and main forks of the Dosewallips River. A second bridge spans the deep chasm of the West Fork, and the waters churn through a turbulent passage far below it. On the canyon rims, a dry forest of western hemlock is underlain by a sparse growth of salal. Pacific rhododendrons are abundant here; watch for their pink blossoms in May. There are no restraining structures along the lip of the gorge; stay well away from the edge and use the bridge to view the chasm. Return to the trailhead via the same route.

West Fork Dosewallips Gorge

4
MOUNT ZION

Type of hike: Out-and-back.
Total distance: 3.5 miles (round trip).
Elevation gain: 1,340-foot gain.
Time required: 2 to 4 hours.
Maps: USGS Mount Zion; Custom Correct *Buckhorn Wilderness*.
Finding the trailhead: From the Sequim, drive east on U.S. Highway 101 to mile 267.4 and turn south on Palo Alto Road. The pavement ends after 6 miles, and the road becomes Forest Road 28. Drive another 7 miles or so to Forest Road 2810. Turn left and follow this secondary road 2 miles to the marked trailhead. From Quilcene, drive north on US 101 to the Lords Lake Loop Road. Follow this road to FR 28, and drive northwest on this trunk road to reach the junction with FR 2810 at Bon Jon Pass. Turn right and follow FR 2810 the remaining 2 miles to the trailhead.

Key points
0.0   Mount Zion Trailhead.
0.7   Trail reaches overlook rock.
1.8   Summit of Mount Zion.

The hike: This trail offers one of the easiest ascents to a summit in the Olympic Mountains. From its position at the leeward edge of the mountains, views stretch across the

Mount Zion

210

To 28

Mt. Zion
4,278 ft.

2810

Gold Creek

N

0   .5   1   *To* 28

Miles

glittering waters of Puget Sound to the snowy crags of the Cascade Range, with its dormant volcanoes rising high above glacier-carved ridges. The trail does not offer a wilderness setting; Mount Zion lies within the Olympic National Forest and is surrounded by clearcuts. Hikers may have to share the trail with motorbikes (although the narrow trail and bumpy water bars discourage most dirt bikers). The trail is especially spectacular in early July, when the pink blossoms of Pacific rhododendron light up the forests that skirt the peak.

The trail begins by following a forested finger ridge to the base of the mountain, then climbs steadily across the slopes on a northerly heading. The large, shiny leaves of the rhododendron crowd the forest understory in these early stretches, and it is here that the best displays of blossoms are to be found. The trail ultimately doglegs to the southeast, climbing beneath basalt monoliths that rise from the wooded slopes. One of the tallest outcrops yields westward views of Gray Wolf Ridge, capped by a row of impressive peaks.

Just below the summit, the trail embarks upon a series of tight switchbacks. The trail ends in a grassy clearing on the mountaintop. While views of the Olympic Mountains are screened by the trees, a broad panorama of Puget Sound stretches below. To the northeast, the snowy cone of Mount Baker and its smaller neighbor, Mount Shuksan, rise beyond Discovery and Sequim bays. Far to the southeast, Mount Rainier soars skyward, its glistening glaciers dwarfing the wooded ridges that surround it. Retrace the trail back to the trailhead to complete the hike.

Hurricane Ridge

OVERVIEW

The high alpine meadows of Hurricane Ridge are easily reached from Port Angeles via a paved road and are extremely popular with day hikers. The entire length of Hurricane Ridge from Obstruction Point to Hurricane Hill escaped glaciation during the ice ages, serving as a refuge for alpine plants and animals. The result is an outstanding diversity of wildflowers, featuring several species that are found nowhere else in the world. There are excellent opportunities for wildlife viewing, particularly blacktail deer and Olympic marmots, in the extensive alpine meadows.

The main visitor center for Olympic National Park is located at the beginning of the Hurricane Ridge Road at the southern edge of Port Angeles. A smaller visitor center is sited in the meadows atop Hurricane Ridge, and ranger-guided interpretive walks are organized from this point. The more primitive Obstruction Point Road, a narrow gravel road with pullouts that are not suited to motor homes or trailers but can be negotiated by most passenger cars, departs near this point. This road is cleared of snow in July and closes at the end of September. The Deer Park Road is a similar gravel trunk road that climbs steeply from the coastal plains east of Port Angeles to the mountaintops. There are auto campgrounds at Deer Park as well as Heart 'o the Hills, which is just inside the park boundary on the Hurricane Ridge Road. All services can be found in the towns of Port Angeles and Sequim.

Hurricane Ridge

5
HEART O' THE FOREST TRAIL

Type of hike: Out-and-back.
Total distance: 4.1 miles (round trip).
Elevation change: 200-foot loss.
Time required: 2 to 3.5 hours.
Maps: USGS Port Angeles; Custom Correct *Hurricane Ridge*.
Finding the trailhead: From the park visitor center in Port Angeles, drive 6.4 miles up the Hurricane Ridge Road to Heart o' the Hills Campground. The trail begins from a marked trailhead on Campground Loop E.

The hike: This 2-mile trail leads into the forest to the east of the Heart 'o the Hills Campground. It offers no mountain views, but does travel through some of the most stately old-growth forest on the Olympic Peninsula. This ancient woodland is made up of silver fir, redcedar, and Douglas-fir, with some of the largest trees exceeding 8 feet in diameter. Old trees often die from the top down, and the broken-topped giants provide the unique nesting habitat for the northern spotted owl, one of the most celebrated and controversial of our endangered species.

The trail stays fairly level for the majority of its length, where numerous rills are choked with the giant leaves of devils club and skunk cabbage. As the widely spaced giants give way to a younger stand of hemlock and Douglas-fir, the path descends steadily into a narrow creek valley. The trail ends rather ignominiously at the park boundary, where the forest has been clearcut right up to the edge of the park, swallowing up the trail in the process. Turn around here to complete the hike.

Heart o' the Forest Trail

6
HURRICANE RIDGE LOOPS

Type of hike: A series of loops.
Total distance: 0.3 mile to 1.5 miles, depending on route.
Elevation change: Minimal to 200-foot gain, depending on route.
Time required: 20 minutes to 1.5 hours, depending on route.
Maps: USGS Mount Angeles; Custom Correct *Hurricane Ridge*.
Finding the trailhead: From Port Angeles, drive 17.6 miles south on the Hurricane Ridge Road to the visitor center atop the ridge. The trails depart from the northeast corner of the parking lot.

The hike: A network of walking trails wanders through the subalpine meadows atop Hurricane Ridge. This popular area receives more visitors than any other spot within the park, and because of the heavy foot traffic, most of the trails have been paved. The sole exception is the High Ridge Loop, which is graveled and has a more challenging grade than the other trails, which are quite easy. All of the trails offer outstanding views of the mountains, including Mount Olympus when the weather cooperates. A startling diversity of wildflowers offers a different combination of blossoms with each passing week. Mule deer and Olympic marmots are abundant here, and they are unafraid of humans. (Do not feed them!) There is a visitor center across the parking lot, and guided ranger walks are offered on a periodic basis. Each trail within the network will be discussed separately. The author's favorite routing follows the Cirque Rim Trail, with a side trip up the High Ridge Loop for an overall hike of 1.3 miles.

Big Meadow Loop. This short loop wanders through the lush meadows beside the parking lot. Though crowded, this trail offers the best opportunities to view wildlife and alpine flowers. A broad panorama of the Olympic Mountains spans the horizon to the south.

Cirque Rim Trail. This trail follows the northern edge of Hurricane Ridge, passing through copses of subalpine fir and secluded glades. A spur path descends from its westernmost point to reach an overlook of the Little River

Hurricane Ridge Loops

To Port Angeles

To Hurricane Hill

N

To Obstruction Point

0   .5   1

Miles

valley, which is guarded by Hurricane Hill, Unicorn Peak, and Griff Peak. As the main trail follows the rim of a glacial cirque, openings reveal northward vistas that encompass the Strait of Juan de Fuca and Vancouver Island rising beyond it. During clear weather, both Port Angeles and Victoria, B.C., are visible. Mount Angeles is the prominent summit to the east, while below the trail is a ski lift that serves cross-country skiers during the winter months. Upon reaching it, the Cirque Rim Trail turns south; follow it downward through the meadows to return to the parking lot.

High Ridge Loop. This 0.5-mile hike begins at the north-east corner of the Big Meadow Loop and ascends a steep ridgeline. It soon reaches a level overlook that commands excellent views. The Lillian River valley stretches southward, far below, with snow-dappled peaks on both sides. The next valley to the west bears the Elwha River, and beyond it are the Bailey Range and Mount Olympus itself. The pavement ends here, and now a gravel walkway completes the moderate ascent to the crest of a rocky knoll. The path then descends to a junction with Sunrise Point and Mount Angeles trails (the latter is a longer trek and is discussed on page 32). Take a hard left to continue the loop hike, which descends rather steeply through a subalpine woodland. Turn left at the top of the ski lift, where a paved path leads across the Big Meadow and back to the parking lot.

Sunrise Point Spur. This short side path ascends from the High Ridge Trail to the top of a stony knob. With a little jockeying for position, one can have views in all directions, featuring the Bailey Range and Mount Olympus to the southwest, Unicorn Peak to the west, and Steeple Rock to the southeast with the broad and snowy massif of Elk Mountain beyond it.

7
MOUNT ANGELES

Type of hike: Shuttle.
Total distance: 3.4 miles.
Elevation change: 520-foot gain, 1,320-foot loss.
Time required: 1.5 to 3 hours.
Maps: USGS Mount Angeles; Custom Correct *Hurricane Ridge*.
Finding the trailhead: From Port Angeles, drive 17.6 miles south on the Hurricane Ridge Road to the lodge atop the ridge. The hike begins on the High Ridge Trail, which departs from the northeast corner of the parking lot. The trail ends at the Switchback Trailhead (also known as the Third Peak parking area), 3 miles down the Hurricane Ridge Road from the Hurricane Ridge Visitor Center.

Key points:

0.0   Hurricane Ridge parking area.
0.4   Mount Angeles Trail departs from High Ridge Trail.
2.2   Way Trail toward summit. Bear right.
2.7   Junction with Switchback Trail. Turn right to begin descent.
3.4   Trail reaches Hurricane Ridge Road at the Switchback Trail parking area.

The hike: This hike begins in the tourist-thronged meadows atop Hurricane Ridge, but the crowds thin out abruptly as the trail ventures eastward through the spectacular meadows on the shoulders of Klahhane Ridge. Virtually the entire trek is at or above timberline, and wildflower displays are often impressive. Superb vistas encompass the heart of the Olympic Mountains, with the glacier-clad summit of Mount Olympus presiding above the lesser crags.

The trip begins in the complex of paved nature trails on Hurricane Ridge. Follow the High Ridge Trail northeastward as it climbs through alpine meadows. The junction with the Mount Angeles Trail is just beyond the first knob on the ridgetop. This path rises and falls, tracking the

Mount Angeles

ridgetop northeastward through alpine meadows interrupted by stands of perfectly conical subalpine firs. There are wildflowers of all varieties here, highlighted by lupines, larkspurs, bistorts, and a magenta variety of paintbrush that is endemic to the Olympics. To the south lies a sea of snowcapped peaks. The rugged Bailey Range partially screens Mount Olympus to the southwest, while Steeple Rock rises in front of Elk Mountain farther east.

When the trail reaches the base of Mount Angeles, an unmarked climber's trail shoots straight up toward the summit. Bear right as the main trail runs beneath the twisted basalt spires that guard the flanks of the peak. The path soon makes a shallow descent to intercept the Switchback Trail.

Dedicated hikers will want to climb up to the saddle in Klahhane Ridge, which overlooks a nameless basin guarded by rugged ridges. (This fairly strenuous side trip adds 1.9 miles to the length of the trek). There is a good possibility of sighting marmots and chipmunks on the ridgetop. More rarely, mountain goats, and black bears are spotted in the basin or among the rocks above it. Hardy alpine plants like spreading phlox and creeping penstemon brighten the rockscape.

Visitors who are pressed for time can hike directly down the Switchback Trail to regain the road far below the starting point. A foot-pounding series of switchbacks leads down the mountainside, passing copses of fir and mountain hemlock en route to the Third Peak parking area.

8
HURRICANE HILL

Type of hike: Out-and-back.
Total distance: 2.9 miles (round trip).
Elevation change: 660-foot gain.
Time required: 1.5 to 3 hours.
Maps: USGS Hurricane Hill; Custom Correct *Hurricane Ridge*.
Finding the trailhead: From Port Angeles, drive south 18.9 miles on the Hurricane Ridge Road. The hike begins at the road's end, where a parking area marks the trailhead.

Key points:
0.0   Trailhead.
0.4   Junction with Little River Trail. Keep going straight.
1.4   Spur trail to summit of Hurricane Hill.
1.5   Summit of Hurricane Hill.

The hike: This trail offers a scenic walk to a grassy summit at the western end of Hurricane Ridge. Most of the tourists never get farther than the Hurricane Ridge Visitor Center; if you take the extra drive out to Hurricane Hill, you can enjoy the same beautiful meadows, mountain wildlife, and spectacular vistas without the crowds. This route follows a paved nature trail with interpretive plaques, and though it does have some ups and downs, it is wheelchair accessible

Hurricane Hill

for the first half mile.

The hike begins with a gradual climb along a flower-strewn ridgeline. There are outstanding views of the Bailey Range here, and black-tailed deer and Olympic marmots are sometimes sighted. The trail soon reaches a saddle where the stark and forbidding heights of Mount Angeles can be seen to the east. The Little River Trail drops from this low pass into the valley to the north. The main path continues to climb the grassy flanks of Hurricane Hill, reaching a second junction near the top. To the right, the paved trail runs 0.2 mile to the summit of the hill, which overlooks a shallow alpine tarn and provides good views of Unicorn Peak. The broader panorama encompasses the Strait of Juan de Fuca and Canada to the north and the regal summit of Mount Olympus to the south. Turn around here to complete the hike.

9
ELK MOUNTAIN

Type of hike: Shuttle.
Total distance: 7.4 miles.
Elevation change: 1,260-foot gain, 2,120-foot loss.
Time required: 4 to 7 hours.
Maps: USGS Mount Angeles; Custom Correct *Gray Wolf-Dosewallips*
Finding the trailhead: From Port Angeles, drive 17.6 miles south on the Hurricane Ridge Road to the visitor center parking lot. Turn sharply left (south) onto the narrow, winding Obstruction Point Road. This route is too narrow for trailers and RVs. Drive 7.6 miles to road's end at Obstruction Point. The trail begins at the north end of the parking area. The hike ends at the ranger station at Deer Park.

Key points:
0.0   Obstruction Point Trailhead
0.2   Junction with Badger Valley Trail. Keep going straight.
2.0   Junction with cutoff trail to Badger Valley. Bear left.
2.6   Easternmost summit of Elk Mountain.
3.2   Roaring Winds Pass.
3.9   Maiden Peak.
7.4   Deer Park Ranger Station.

The hike: This trail offers a point-to-point hike across alpine ridges from Obstruction Point in the west to Deer Park Campground in the east. Water is scarce along this route, so be sure to bring along a plentiful supply. A steep snowfield may block the beginning of the Elk Mountain Trail. An ice ax may be required before mid-July.

The trail begins by crossing a grassy bowl that is home to a marmot colony; the engaging behavior of these social rodents can entertain you for hours. The path drops across the steep headwall of the Badger Valley as it rounds Obstruction Peak, and the Badger Valley Trail drops away to the

Elk Mountain

right. Continue straight on the Elk Mountain Trail. The path then begins to ascend onto the broad summit of Elk Mountain, with its endless rocky fells sprinkled with the blossoms of phlox and dwarf lupine. The rocky interstices support a sparse growth of hardy lichens that are close cousins to the ones that provide Arctic caribou herds with their winter forage. Take a glance backward for a grandstand view of the heart of the Olympic Mountains, from Mount Christie in the south to the Bailey Range in the north, and surmounted by the ice-bound mass of Mount Olympus itself. To the south, the glacier-clad summit of Mount Cameron is partially hidden by the ridges that rise above the Grand Valley. The ragged spires of The Needles rise farther to the east.

As Elk Mountain peters out, the trail descends steeply to reach Roaring Winds Pass. The trail then climbs high onto the flanks of Maiden Peak. The south slope of this peak is quite arid and supports a rather sparse flora of grasses and lichens interspersed with bistorts and dwarf lupines. A short trek to the ridgeline allows the traveler to look down into the basin containing Maiden Lake, a small, shallow pool of pale aquamarine. The slopes of Maiden Peak offer the park's finest view of The Needles, which are, from north to south, Mount Walkinshaw, Mount Clark, and Mount Johnson. Mount Deception is the southernmost summit on this craggy ridge.

The path rounds the rocky eastern spur of Maiden Peak, then descends through rolling tundra as the subalpine firs close in around the ridgeline. Moist glades support white and pink heathers, avalanche lilies, and a deep lavender variety of paintbrush. As the trail drops onto the south slope of Green Mountain, it enters an arid forest of lodgepole pine. There is little in the way of understory vegetation here, and this habitat type is avoided by most species of wildlife. After a rather long and jolting descent into a low saddle, the trail picks up an old roadbed that climbs the remaining distance to reach the hike's end at the Deer Park Ranger Station. Hikers who do not have a vehicle waiting should turn around here to complete the hike.

10
LILLIAN RIDGE

Type of hike: Out-and-back.
Total distance: 3.2 miles (round trip).
Elevation change: 510-foot gain, 170-foot loss to turn-around point.
Time required: 1.5 to 3 hours.
Maps: USGS Mount Angeles; Custom Correct *Gray Wolf-Dosewallips*.
Finding the trailhead: From Port Angeles, drive 17.6 miles south on the Hurricane Ridge Road to the visitor center parking lot. Turn sharply left (south) onto the narrow, winding Obstruction Point Road. This route is too narrow for trailers and RVs. Drive 7.6 miles to the road's end at Obstruction Point. The trail runs south from the parking area.

The hike: This outstanding ridge trek follows Lillian Ridge, an alpine divide that offer views of sparkling lakes and a broad sweep of the eastern Olympics.

The trail begins at Obstruction Point, where a colony of marmots has excavated a network of tunnels. Their playful antics are on display for anyone who can remain inconspicuous for a while. The trail soon climbs onto the rounded top of Lillian Ridge, clad in lush meadows that grade into an arid alpine tundra. This is an alpine desert in which hardy flowers such as dwarf lupine, phlox, and fleabane eke out a hardscrabble existence in the gusting winds, short growing seasons, and lack of water found here. Spectacular scenery stretches in all directions. To the east, the Needles rise sheer above the intervening ridgetops. To the south, McCartney Peak rises above the Lillian River valley amid a sea of equally spectacular (though nameless) summits, and the omnipresent mass of Mount Olympus hulks to the west.

Lillian Ridge

After 1.6 miles of up-and-down travel, the trail drops into a low saddle. A climber's trail continues along the ridgeline to the south, while the main path bends east to descend into the Grand Valley. The blue mirror of Grand Lake can be seen far below amid verdant forests on the valley floor. The alpine desert is particularly barren in this area: low-growing krummholz fir huddle in small clumps amid wide expanses of bare, rocky soil. These shrublike conifers are actually the same species as the spire-shaped firs that grow in more protected locales. When a young tree takes root on an exposed ridgetop like this one, the winter gales blow snow and particles of ice across the surface of the snowdrifts, abrading away any branches that rise above the snow line. Over time, this natural pruning creates a ground-hugging mat of branches that may represent a tree that is hundreds of years old.

Enjoy the beauty of the alpine scenery, pack a lunch for a sublime dining experience in the wilds, search for rodents on the surrounding slopes and raptors in the skies. Be conscious of the fragility of this high alpine environment, and confine your activities to bare rock. After taking in the delights, retrace your steps to complete the hike.

The Elwha River

OVERVIEW

The valley of the Elwha River penetrates to the geographic center of the park, a deep, glacier-carved trough in the midst of crags. The Elwha band of S'Klallams once had a village along the Elwha's banks, since flooded by the waters of Lake Mills. Fierce hunters from this band ranged far up the valley in pursuit of elk.

Later, members of the Press Expedition chose this corridor in their crossing of the range. This ragtag band of booze hounds and glory seekers required two months to trace the Elwha to its source and follow the North Fork of the Quinault down to civilization. (The same journey today, with the assistance of good trails, takes four or five days.) Along the way, the Press Expedition named many of the austere crags at the heart of the Olympics for the obscure newspaper barons who funded their expedition. In the late 1800s, homesteading activity occurred in the Geyser Valley part of the drainage, and several sturdy cabins remain to this day. Olympic Hot Springs, once a developed resort, has been returned to a natural state and offers a undeveloped alternative to Sol Duc Hot Springs.

Both the Hurricane Ridge and Olympic Hot Springs roads have fee entrance stations on them. There is a full-fledged visitor center in Port Angeles and a ranger station in the Elwha Valley. There is camping at the Elwha and Altaire campgrounds in the Elwha Valley. Port Angeles offers all services required by the traveler, and there are limited supplies at the junction of U.S. Highway 101 and Olympic Hot Springs Road.

The Elwha River

11
MADISON CREEK FALLS

Type of hike: Out-and-back.
Total distance: 0.2 mile (round trip).
Elevation change: Mimimal
Time required: 10 to 20 minutes.
Maps: USGS Elwha; Custom Correct *Hurricane Ridge*.
Finding the trailhead: Take U.S. Highway 101 west from Port Angeles, then follow Olympic Hot Springs Road south up the Elwha Valley. The Madison Creek Falls Trail begins from the parking area beside the entrance station.

The hike: This paved pathway offers a gentle stroll on the floor of the Elwha River valley, visiting a stunning waterfall hidden at the edge of the valley. The trail is suited to all visitors and accommodates wheelchairs with ease. It begins near the Elwha River entrance station and wanders eastward across grassy meadows to reach an impressive waterfall on Madison Creek. Here, the stream drops across a sheer cliff to reach the valley floor, and a lush mixture of hardwoods thrives in the abundant moisture of this pleasant pocket in the foothills. From the waterfall, turn around to return to the parking area.

Madison Creek Falls

12
GEYSER VALLEY LOOP

Type of hike: Loop.
Total distance: 5.6 miles.
Elevation change: 380-foot gain, 380-foot loss overall.
Time required: 3 to 5 hours.
Maps: USGS Hurricane Hill, Custom Correct *Elwha Valley*.
Finding the trailhead: From U.S. Highway 101, follow Olympic Hot Springs Road up the Elwha Valley. Just beyond the ranger station, turn left onto Whiskey Bend Road. Follow this narrow, winding gravel road 4.4 miles to the trailhead at its end.

Key points:
0.0 Whiskey Bend Trailhead. Follow the Elwha River Trail southeast.
0.9 Spur path descends to "Eagle's Nest Overlook." Visit the overlook and then continue southeast on the Elwha River Trail.
1.2 Junction with Rica Canyon Trail. Stay left on Elwha River Trail.
1.6 Junction with Krause Bottom Trail. Stay left on Elwha River Trail.
1.9 Michael's Cabin and junction with Humes Ranch Trail. Turn right.
2.1 Junction with Dodger Point Trail. Bear right.

2.3   Humes Ranch. Turn right onto the Geyser Valley Trail,
      following signs for Krause Bottom.
3.0   Junction with Krause Bottom Trail. Visit Krause
      homestead site, then hike west toward the Rica Can-
      yon Trail.
3.9   Junction with Goblin Gates Spur Trail. Hike to over-
      look (0.2-mile round trip), then ascend on Rica Can-
      yon Trail.
4.4   Junction with Elwha River Trail. Turn left to finish
      the hike.
5.6   Hike ends at Whiskey Bend Trailhead.

The hike: This pleasant hike visits the bottomlands along the
lower reaches of the Elwha River. The earliest white explor-
ers to visit this area named it the Geyser Valley, fooled
perhaps by swirling mists and the drumming of grouse into
believing that there were thermal geysers in the area. At the
turn of the 20th century, a small number of homesteaders
moved into the area, building rustic cabins with the abundant local timber and clearing small patches of forest to plant
their gardens. The homesteads have long been abandoned,
but a few old cabins remain to delight the modern visitor.
This loop trip also visits the Goblin Gates, a striking geological feature that marks the head of Rica Canyon.

From Whiskey Bend Trailhead, the trail runs southward
along a forested hillside high above the valley floor. A spur
path soon runs down to an overlook named the "Eagle's Nest
Overlook" by the Press Expedition. This spot commands a
fine view of the Elwha Valley, and the meadows of the former
Anderson homestead can be seen across the river. Elk and

black bear are sometimes seen in this bottomland clearing during the morning or evening. The trail then makes its way across the several burns of the 1977 Rica Canyon fire. The fire site is recovering naturally with a dense growth of shrubs and saplings. The Rica Canyon Trail drops away in the middle of the first burn; follow the Elwha River Trail to the left. At the far edge of the burn is a junction with the Krause Bottom Trail.

Bear left to reach Michael's Cabin, one of the many Geyser Valley homesteads. This sturdy dwelling was once the property of a colorful resident known locally as "Cougar Mike," a nemesis of mountain lions noted for his sharp-

Geyser Valley Loop

shooting ability. The next meadow to the north is the former site of Geyser House, a ramshackle hostelry that was run by a former Seattle policeman known as "Doc" Ludden. This self-proclaimed "Bee Man of the Elwha" kept hives of honeybees and made his own honey.

The loop route now departs from the Elwha River Trail, descending toward the river bottoms on the Humes Ranch Trail. This trail descends obliquely through the trees, passing a junction with the Dodger Point Trail (bear right here). It then crosses diminutive Antelope Creek and descends sharply to reach the Humes Ranch after 0.4 mile. The cabin found here was built by Grant and Will Humes in 1900, who were among the earliest homesteaders in the Elwha Valley. This dynamic pair of brothers ran an outfitting operation in the Olympic Mountains, running pack trains for expeditions of climbers, hunters, and sightseers.

A junction with the Geyser Valley Trail marked "Krause Bottom" lies at the lower edge of the clearing; bear right onto this trail to continue the loop hike. This trail descends to the lush river flats. Here clumps of gnarled vine maple are draped with mosses, and a mixed forest of red alder and Douglas-fir provides a rather sparse canopy. After 0.7 mile, the Geyser Valley Trail rises to an elevated terrace to meet the Krause Bottom Trail.

The loop hike continues along the Geyser Valley Trail, but first take a brief stroll up the Krause Bottom Trail to visit the old Krause homestead. It occupies a meadowy bench sprinkled with ornamental fruit trees that have reverted to a more or less wild state. These trees are the remnants of the Krause orchard. It was planted by a German couple who homesteaded here in the mid-1890s, but a fire burned them out and they were forced to abandon their pioneering efforts. The clearing and orchard trees are the only trace that remains of their labors.

After visiting the Krause homestead site, hike west on the Geyser Valley Trail. It drops back into a quiet riverbottom forest, where the murmur of the river provides a soothing background for the twittering of birds. A luxuriant undergrowth of moss, vanilla leaf, and sword fern suffuses the forest with a soft green light. The trail emerges for the first time beside the Elwha River at an outcrop of unyielding stone that receives the full force of the water.

Just beyond this spot is the spur trail that follows the river downstream for 0.1 mile to an outcrop of bedrock that overlooks Goblin Gates. This interesting geological formation marks the entrance to Rica Canyon. It is an uplift of slate and sandstone that has been riven by the swirling turquoise waters of the Elwha over the course of centuries. The name reflects the imagination of early visitors who thought that they could discern the craggy faces of goblins amid the folds and crenellations of the rock walls.

To complete the loop, walk back to the Goblin Gates junction and follow the Rica Canyon Trail eastward across a forested terrace. It soon begins a stiff climb to meet the Elwha River Trail, zigzagging upward for 0.5 mile as it enters the Rica Canyon burn once more. Upon reaching the Elwha River Trail, turn left and retrace the initial leg of the hike to return to Whiskey Bend.

13
OLYMPIC HOT SPRINGS

Type of hike: Out-and-back.
Total distance: 4.9 miles (round trip).
Elevation change: 190-foot gain, 60-foot loss to springs.
Time required: 2.5 to 4 hours (add more time if you want to take a dip).
Maps: USGS Mount Carrie; Custom Correct *Lake Crescent-Happy Lake Ridge.*
Finding the trailhead: From U.S. Highway 101 west of Port Angeles, follow the Olympic Hot Springs Road, which ascends the Elwha Valley into the park. Stay on the main road as you pass the Elwha Ranger Station, go past the Altaire Campground, and continue up the road to the parking area and trailhead at the end of the road.

Key points:
0.0   Boulder Creek Trailhead.
2.2   Junction with Olympic Hot Springs Spur Trail. Bear left.
2.3   Trail crosses bridge over Boulder Creek to access first of the hot pools.
2.4   Uppermost hot pool.

The hike: This old roadbed follows Boulder Creek up to the undeveloped hot springs on its south bank. The hot springs are quite popular with local weekenders; visit them during the week to avoid the crowds. These hot pools are not tested for the presence of pathogens; bathe at your own risk.

For the first 2.2 miles the trek follows an old paved road along the forested banks of Boulder Creek. A second-growth forest of Douglas-fir shades the old road, and slide alders are beginning to encroach along its edges. This road ends at a junction below the Boulder Creek Campground. The path to Olympic Hot Springs continues upstream along the creek,

Olympic Hot Springs

then crosses it and turns back to the east to reach the hot pools. There was once a developed resort here, but it has long since been torn down. The pools have been returned to a natural state and are scattered across the hillside above the stream. Each pool has its own temperature, and the lowest pools have mud bottoms while the upper pools are lined with rock. After visiting the pools, retrace the trail back to the trailhead.

Lake Crescent
and the Sol Duc River

OVERVIEW

This northern fringe of the Olympic Mountains is dominated by heavily forested peaks. The low basins were originally carved by glaciers and now bear the drainages of the Lyre and Sol Duc rivers. *Sol Duc* means "sparkling waters" in the dialect of the S'Klallams, and this great stream is born in an area of tremendous geothermal activity. Waters heated by molten magma rise through faults in the Juan de Fuca Plate, leaking to the surface at Sol Duc Hot Springs. These waters have been harnessed in swimming pool form at a full-scale resort within the park.

Lake Crescent is one of the primary attractions of the area. This large body of water is clear and cold, surrounded by imposing peaks. This lake attained its present size when a landslide blocked its eastern outlet, and the water level rose until it poured over the northern lip of the basin to form the Lyre River. This new outlet stream was too turbulent to admit the passage of sea-run rainbow and cutthroat trout that inhabited the lake, and these isolated stocks evolved into the beardslee and crescenti trout, respectively.

There are ranger stations near Sol Duc Hot Springs and on Barnes Point on the south shore of Lake Crescent. The Sol Duc Hot Springs Resort, Lake Crescent Lodge, and Log Cabin Resort provide lodgings within the national park, and there are campgrounds near the hot springs and at the western end of Lake Crescent. An entrance fee is charged on Sol Duc Hot Springs Road. The Fairholm general store at the western end of Lake Crescent and the Sol Duc Hot Springs camp store are the only nearby source of supplies.

Lake Crescent and the Sol Duc River

14
MARYMERE FALLS

Type of hike: Out-and-back.
Total distance: 1.8 miles (round trip).
Elevation change: 80-foot gain.
Time required: 1 to 1.5 hours.
Maps: USGS Lake Crescent; Custom Correct *Lake Crescent–Happy Lake Ridge*.
Finding the trailhead: Take U.S. Highway 101 to mile 228 on the south shore of Lake Crescent, then take a short side road north to the Storm King Ranger Station. The trail begins from this point and crosses underneath the highway.

Key points:
0.0   Storm King Ranger Station.
0.4   Trail is joined by a cutoff trail from the Lake Crescent Lodge.
0.5   Storm King Trail departs to the left. Stay right, on the main trail.
0.7   Marymere Falls Trail splits away from Barnes Creek Trail. Turn right and cross log footbridge over Barnes Creek.
0.9   Trail reaches viewing platform at the base of Marymere Falls.

The hike: From the shores of Lake Crescent, this trail offers a short trip into a beautiful old-growth forest of Douglas-fir,

Marymere Falls

then crosses Barnes Creek and climbs a steep stairway to Marymere Falls, a 90-foot cascade. There are interpretive signs along the way, and the forest portion of the trail can be readily negotiated by wheelchairs.

To begin the hike, follow the paved pathway that runs south from the ranger station. It soon ducks through an underpass beneath the highway, emerging among the tall columns of a Douglas-fir forest. This a true old-growth stand, and new seedlings can take root only as the most ancient trees die of old age and fall to the forest floor, creating sunny openings in the canopy. The vigor of this stand of trees is due in part to the richness of the alluvial soil, brought down by Barnes Creek and deposited in a delta as the creek waters entered Lake Crescent and slowed to allow their load of silt to settle out.

Upon reaching the upper edge of the delta, there is a junction with the trail that leads up Barnes Creek to Aurora Ridge. Turn right as the Marymere Falls Trail leads to a log footbridge over Barnes Creek. There is a loose woodland of redcedar on the far bank, and here the trail becomes a steep but well-built stairway that leads up to the base of Marymere Falls. The falls is a slender ribbon of water brought down from Aurora Ridge by a tributary stream, and its constant mist supports a growth of ferns and mosses on the surrounding rock. From the viewing platform, turn around to complete the hike.

15
THE SPRUCE RAILROAD TRAIL

Type of hike: Shuttle.
Total distance: 4 miles.
Elevation change: 260-foot gain, 260-foot loss.
Time required: 2 to 3.5 hours.
Maps: USGS Lake Crescent; Custom Correct *Lake Crescent–Happy Lake Ridge*.
Finding the trailhead: Take U.S. Highway 101 to a junction with the East Beach Road, at mile marker 232 just east of Lake Crescent. Follow this winding, paved road 3.2 miles, passing the Log Cabin Resort and turning left on another paved road bearing a sign for the Spruce Railroad Trail. This road crosses the Lyre River to reach a parking area near some private residences. The trail begins from a sign on the west side of the road. The trail ends at the end of the Camp David Jr. Road, which departs from US 101 just west of the Fairholm general store at the western end of Lake Crescent.

Key points:
0.0   East trailhead.
0.8   Harrigan Point.
1.1   Devil's Point.
2.9   Second tunnel.
4.0   West trailhead.

get FALCON GUIDED

FALCONGUIDES are the ultimate in recreational guidebooks. Each guide provides comprehensive information on trails, trips, and the best places to go in each state. Detailed descriptions are accompanied by maps, access information, photos, and safety tips. Regularly updated and revised, FALCONGUIDES provide the most current, accurate information possible. Whatever you do outside, use a FALCONGUIDE to plan your next trip into the great outdoors.

FALCON GUIDES are available for:
Hiking, Rock Climbing, Rockhounding, Mountain Biking, Scenic Driving, Watching Wildlife, Fishing and more.

MORE THAN 4 MILLION COPIES SOLD!

To locate your nearest retailer call
1-800-582-2665.
Also use this number for a complete list of Falcon titles including books on nature and the West. **For a FREE catalog, return this card with the following information.**

Name _____
Address _____
City _____
State _____ Zip _____

☐ **YES!** I'd like to send a catalog to a friend.

Name _____
Address _____
City _____
State _____ Zip _____

FALCON

FALCON®

BUSINESS REPLY MAIL

FIRST-CLASS MAIL   PERMIT NO. 80   HELENA MT

POSTAGE WILL BE PAID BY THE ADDRESSEE

FALCON PUBLISHING CO INC
PO BOX 1718
HELENA MT 59624-9917

The Spruce Railroad Trail

The hike: This trail offers a gentle stroll along the north shore of Lake Crescent, making a point-to-point hike that is described here from east to west. It follows an old railbed that was built during World War I to transport Sitka spruce from the then-inaccessible western part of the peninsula to the aircraft factories. Sitka spruce has a superior ratio of strength to weight, and was therefore coveted for the making of biplane airframes. The railroad was completed in a remarkable time of only six weeks, but the war was over before the first logs rolled eastward on the rails. The railway was active through the 1950s, when it was abandoned and subsequently turned into a trail. It is one of the only trails in Olympic National Park where mountain bikes are permitted. For hikers who lack the time or inclination to hike the entire trail, Devil's Point makes an ideal turn-around point. Watch out for poison oak if you get off the trail.

The trail begins by running inland from North Shore Road, climbing gently to reach the old railroad grade. As the railbed runs southward, it passes through a mixed forest of red alder and Douglas-fir, skirting inland to avoid private residences along the lakeshore. It then descends to the shoreline, although dense trees screen out views of the water. A rough spur path to Harrigan Point brings the traveler to a grassy spit that offers the first unobstructed vistas of the hike.

A short distance farther, the main trail climbs a bit to round the rocky headland of Devil's Point. A tunnel was blasted through the bedrock of the point to accommodate the railway, but it has since been sealed off with rocky debris. The point itself offers fine views of the north arm of the lake and Mount Storm King rising above the waters to the south. Pacific madrones thrive in the thin soils of this sunny locale. A bridge soon arches above the waters of a narrow and rocky cove. The imposing rock faces that rise all around this inlet are the exposed foundation of Pyramid Peak.

Just beyond the bridge are fine views of the western arm of the lake, with the towering green wall of Aurora Ridge dominating its south shore. The next stretch of shoreline is frequently punctuated by openings where the trail skirts the base of sheer cliffs. Lake Crescent Lodge occupies the alluvial delta of Barnes Creek on the far side of the lake. Soon, the trail reaches a second tunnel, and the eastern entrance of this one has not been blocked. The tunnel is choked with rubble and rotting timber, however, and exploring it would be an unsafe proposition. Beside the trail, sections of old rail are reminiscent of earlier times as the path makes its way through sun-dappled groves of red alder to reach the western trailhead. Just before arriving at the trailhead outhouse, the path departs from the railbed and drops to meet the end of the Camp David Jr. Road.

16
SOL DUC FALLS

Type of hike: Out-and-back.
Total distance: 1.5 miles (round trip).
Elevation change: Minimal.
Time required: 45 minutes to 1.5 hours
Maps: USGS Bogachiel Peak; Custom Correct *Seven Lakes Basin–Hoh*.
Finding the trailhead: From U.S. Highway 101, drive about 13 miles on the Sol Duc Hot Springs Road to a large parking lot at its end. The trail departs from the south end of this lot.

Key points:
0.0   Trailhead.
0.1   Junction with spur from Sol Duc Campground. Continue straight ahead.
0.7   Loop trail splits at Sol Duc Falls shelter. Turn right.
0.8   Bridge spans Sol Duc River at Sol Duc Falls.

The hike: From the trailhead, a broad path winds eastward through the towering bottomland forest. The trail forks at the Sol Duc Falls shelter. Follow the right fork down to the river, where a stout bridge and viewing area allow close inspection of this unusual cataract. As the river wore a channel through the stone of the valley floor it encountered a hard, resistant stratum of stone that is tilted vertically and

62

cuts diagonally across the river channel. Immediately south
of this hard layer was a layer of weak, easily eroded rock
through which the waters soon wore a deep path. The result
is Sol Duc Falls, where the river spills in an angled curtain
across the sill of resistant rock and lands 20 feet below in a
deep cleft. From the bridge, retrace the path to return to the
trailhead.

Sol Duc Falls

17
LOVER'S LANE

Type of hike: Loop.
Total distance: 6 miles.
Elevation change: Minimal.
Time required: 2.5 to 4.5 hours.
Maps: USGS Bogachiel Peak; Custom Correct *Seven Lakes Basin–Hoh*.
Finding the trailhead: From U.S. Highway 101, drive about 12 miles on the Sol Duc Hot Springs Road to the Sol Duc Hot Springs Resort. The trek begins and ends at a marked trailhead beside the resort at the western edge of the parking lot.

Key points:
0.0   Lover's Lane Trailhead.
0.1   Junction with trail to Mink Lake. Bear left on wider path.
2.9   Junction with trail to Deer Lake and the High Divide. Turn left.
3.0   Bridge over Sol Duc River at Sol Duc Falls.
3.1   Shelter and junction with trail that follows Sol Duc River. Bear left.
3.7   Junction with trail to Sol Duc Campground Loops. Turn left onto it.
5.1   Trail leaves Campground Loop B at site 62.
5.3   Trail leaves Campground Loop A at site 21.
5.5   Trail passes amphitheater.

5.8   Trail emerges onto road. Turn left and follow road to
      Sol Duc Hot Springs.

6.0   Hike ends at Lover's Lane Trailhead.

The hike: This trail links Sol Duc Hot Springs with Sol Duc Falls, offering an easy loop of 6 miles through the pristine old growth and the auto campgrounds. The forest here mixes the elements of the rainforests to the west with plants of the rainshadow country to the east.

The trail begins by passing behind the swimming pools of Sol Duc Hot Springs. Early in the trek, ranks of moss-draped vine maple arch over the path, while nurse logs and old stumps provide aerial platforms for mosses and seedlings. Near the falls, the more open woodland is dominated by Douglas-fir, and broad glades between the trees are populated by bracken, lady, and sword ferns. After 3 miles, the trail reaches spectacular Sol Duc Falls; from this point, the route follows the Sol Duc Falls Trail downstream toward the trailhead, then follows signs to the campground. Then it wanders close to the east bank of the river for more deep forest scenery, crossing through two campground loops (follow the signs) to return to the lodge.

Lover's Lane

The Western Rainforests

OVERVIEW

The westward-flowing rivers of the Olympic Peninsula flow from massive glaciers at the crest of the range and churn through braided channels to reach the Pacific Ocean. Deep, U-shaped valleys receive more than 150 inches of rain each year, giving rise to the ancient temperate rain forests for which the region is famous. Here, trees may be more than 1,000 years old, and every surface—living and dead—is covered with smaller forms of plant life. A few of the western trails penetrate all the way up into alpine regions, offering views of active glaciers that receive up to 20 feet of snow each winter.

The Hoh and Quinault valleys have the best access, and receive the greatest attention from tourists. The Hoh Rainforest has a major visitor center and campground, and a fee station at the park entrance. There are also several free campgrounds outside the park entrance. Lake Quinault is another focal point for visitors, with several resorts along its southern shore. There is a campground and a seasonal ranger station at Graves Creek and on the North Fork of the Quinault River, and the district ranger station is on Lake Quinault North Shore Road. The Forest Service has a visitor center and several campgrounds on the south shore of the lake.

The other river valleys are wilder and more remote, offering a more primitive wilderness experience. There is a

The Western Rainforests

Park Service campground at the end of Queets River Road, while various state agencies administer campgrounds on the South Fork of the Hoh and Bogachiel rivers. Supplies can be procured at Amanda Park, Quinault, or in Forks, and there are also a few stores along Hoh Rainforest Road.

18
SPRUCE NATURE TRAIL

Type of hike: Loop.
Total distance: 1.3 miles.
Elevation change: Minimal.
Time required: 45 minutes to 1.5 hours.
Maps: USGS Mount Tom; Custom Correct *Seven Lakes Basin–Hoh*.
Finding the trailhead: From Forks, drive south on U.S. Highway 101 to mile 178.5. Turn east on paved Hoh River Road. Drive 18 miles to the trailhead and visitor center at road's end.

The hike: One of the two popular interpretive walks in the Hoh Rainforest, this trail visits impressive stands of old-growth Sitka spruce that grow along the Hoh River. Interpretive plaques along the way explain the ecology of the rainforest. It is paved and is accessible to wheelchairs.

This level trek begins from the midpoint of the short visitor center loop path, and soon makes its way to an old river terrace from which the stout boles of spruce and Douglas-fir tower skyward. This is old-growth rainforest at its finest: The ancient conifers are widely spaced, and plenty of sunlight streams through to support the multiple canopy layers of younger trees, tall shrubs, and a rich ground cover of ferns, mosses, and woodland flowers.

As the path approaches the river, it visits old flood channels that are shaded by groves of red alder. This tree is a specialist at colonizing flood-scoured openings, where thin soils and ample sunlight favor alder seedlings over other plants. At the river's edge, the trail turns downstream to follow the braided channels that course across a barren plain of gravel. Geologically, this is a young river, and its swift current pushes a heavy load of gravel down the riverbed, clogging its own channel and forcing the water to seek a new and lower pathway to the sea. After a brief riverside journey, the trail turns inland through a tangle of vine maples draped with spikemoss. The path soon strikes a spring-fed creek and follows it back to the visitor center.

Spruce Nature Trail

19
HALL OF MOSSES
NATURE TRAIL

Type of hike: Loop.
Total distance: 0.8 mile.
Elevation change: 60-foot gain.
Time required: 30 to 60 minutes.
Maps: Mount Tom, Mount Olympus, *Seven Lakes Basin–Hoh*.
Finding the trailhead: From Forks, drive south on U.S. Highway 101 to milepost 178.5. Turn east on paved Hoh River Road. Drive 18 miles to the trailhead and visitor center at road's end.

The hike: This trail forms a loop through the celebrated Hoh Rainforest, visiting a stand of ghostly old bigleaf maples draped with spikemoss. There are signs along the way to enlighten the visitor about the plants of the old-growth forest.

From its beginning on the visitor center loop, the Hall of Mosses Trail climbs briskly to the top of a spruce-clad terrace. Bear left as the trail splits and then makes its way among the trunks of enormous conifers. Nearing the midpoint of the loop, the trail enters groves of bigleaf maple, long streamers of spikemoss hanging from their massive branches. When soaked with rain, the weight of the moss becomes so great that even a stout branch may break off under the strain. Aerial plants like spikemoss, known to ecologists as *epiphytes*, are one of the hallmarks of a true rainforest. Another epiphyte common to this area is the licorice fern, which grows from moss beds on tree trunks and fallen logs. Watch for nurse logs, fallen trees that have become seedbeds for shrubs and seedlings, as the trail makes its way back to the visitor center.

Hall of Mosses Nature Trail

73

20
HOH RIVER

Type of hike: Out-and-back.
Total distance: Up to 10 miles (round trip), depending on turn-around point.
Elevation change: Minimal.
Time required: Up to 8 hours.
Maps: USGS Mount Tom; Custom Correct *Seven Lakes Basin–Hoh*.
Finding the trailhead: From Forks, drive south on U.S. Highway 101 to mile 178.5. Turn east on paved Hoh River Road. Drive 18 miles to the trailhead and visitor center at road's end.

Key points:
0.0   Hoh Rainforest Visitor Center.
0.2   Hoh River Trail departs from Spruce Nature Trail System.
2.5   Twin Creek Falls
2.9   Spur trail to Mount Tom Meadow Trail.
5.0   Five Mile Island campsites mark turn-around point.

The hike: The journey starts on the paved walkway that is shared with the Spruce Nature Trail system. The Hoh River Trail soon splits off to the northeast—a wide, smooth path that runs across the forest duff. The lower portion of the Hoh valley is robed in a magnificent rainforest, where the enormous boles of the Sitka spruce rise like pillars from the verdant forest floor. Mosses, ferns, and conifer seedlings carpet every level spot, including fallen logs and standing stumps. The trail wanders close to the river at times, affording campsites for short-range travelers. It soon crosses a substantial stream, and soon afterward a smaller cousin. At this point, Mount Tom can be glimpsed to the southeast through a curtain of foliage.

Soon afterward, a spur path leads to Tom Creek Meadows, a camping area situated in a grassy grove of red alder on the riverbank. The Hoh River meanders across a broad

Hoh River

bed of outwash gravel, shifting its course after every major storm. Beyond this point, a handful of western redcedars are conspicuously present in the overstory; some attain magnificent proportions. At mile 4.5 the trail crosses a well-drained terrace. Here ancient spruces rise rank on rank with little intervening vegetation to mask the magnificent vertical landscape.

The route then drops to the river bottoms, crossing dry sloughs and tarrying among tall alders and squat, moss-draped vine maples. The Five Mile Island campsites are among the bottomland at mile 5. This is probably the farthest point that a day traveler could comfortably reach. Turn around here to complete the hike.

21
THE SOUTH FORK
OF THE HOH

Type of hike: Out-and-back.
Total distance: 8.0 miles (round trip).
Elevation change: 110-foot gain, 140-foot loss.
Time required: 4 to 7 hours.
Maps: USGS Mount Tom, Custom Correct *Mount Olympus Climber's Map.*
Finding the trailhead: From mile 176 on U.S. Highway 101 (just south of the Hoh Oxbow Campground), turn southeast on paved Clearwater Road. Drive 8 miles and turn left at signs for the South Fork Campground. Follow markers for Road 1000 (avoid other marked turnoffs) for 10 miles, past the South Fork Hoh Campground, to the trailhead at road's end.

Key points:
0.0   Trailhead.
0.5   Olympic National Park boundary and registration station.
1.5   Trail enters Big Flat.
4.0   End of trail.

The hike: This remote trail offers a quiet stroll through the rainforest and big timber along the South Fork of the Hoh

River. The bottomlands of the South Fork are typified by grassy meadows and thickets of hardwoods. A few ancient conifers rise over all. Due to its remoteness, the South Fork of the Hoh receives relatively few visitors and thus is a good rainforest destination for solitude seekers.

From the trailhead, the path descends through a stand of young spruce, passing a hairpin turn on a closed logging road before veering away to the east. The forest is less dense beyond the park boundary, with a complex overstory featur-

The South Fork of the Hoh

ing a variety of canopy heights. Huge Sitka spruce and western hemlock tower above all, while their younger relatives vie for openings in the canopy. Vine maple is a common understory shrub here, and a variety of forbs and ferns decorate the forest floor.

The descent continues past a fair-sized stream before dropping the traveler onto Big Flat, a broad swath of bottomland on the north bank of the South Fork. Potential campsites abound as the trail continues eastward just out of sight of the river. Ancient spruce trees are spaced hundreds of feet apart, with an understory sometimes crowded with red alder and vine maple and at other times almost entirely absent. The path swings next to an overlook of the river, then crosses through a dense growth of salmonberry on its way inland again. Higher, well-drained benches support stands of Sitka spruce that commonly exceed 10 feet in diameter.

As the path nears the river once again, grassy savannahs separate the conifers and render the trail difficult to detect. It can be followed, however, beyond the next river overlook that features views of Hoh Peak. After crossing a considerable amount of deadfall, the trail peters out on the eastern end of the flats. A hillside descends steeply to meet the river here, blocking further progress to the east. Turn around here to complete the hike.

22
MAPLE GLADE NATURE TRAIL

Type of hike: Loop.
Total distance: 0.5 mile.
Elevation change: Minimal.
Time required: 20 to 45 minutes.
Maps: USGS Finley Creek (trail not shown); Custom Correct *Quinault–Colonel Bob.*
Finding the trailhead: From Amanda Park drive north on U.S. 101 to the Lake Quinault North Shore Road. Follow this paved road east for 6 miles to reach the Lake Quinault Ranger Station (NPS). The hike begins opposite the ranger station.

The hike: This self-guided trail begins next to the Quinault Ranger Station and loops through the lush rainforest bottomlands beside Kestner Creek. A self-guiding pamphlet is available at the beginning of the trail and offers further insights into rainforest ecology.

The trail begins by crossing Kestner Creek. Coarse gravels have been deposited here during floods, creating a well-drained soil that favors the bigleaf maple. Enormous specimens of this rainforest hardwood grow here, their gnarled branches draped with long streamers of spikemoss. Watch for the ubiquitous banana slug, which thrives here on an abundance of hardwood leaf litter.

The maples are interspersed with a few graceful old hemlocks and Sitka spruces, while dense groves of red alder occupy areas of disturbance by fire or flooding. These bottoms serve as winter range for the Roosevelt elk, which mold the forest ecosystem by browsing away young trees and shrubs to create a more open understory. The result of their foraging efforts is a parklike woodland underlain by ground-hugging oxalis, violets, and buttercups.

Maple Glade Nature Trail

23
IRELY LAKE

Type of hike: Out-and-back.
Total distance: 2.6 miles (round trip).
Elevation change: Minimal.
Time required: 1.5 to 3 hours.
Maps: USGS Mount Christie; Custom Correct *Quinault–Colonel Bob*.
Finding the trailhead: Take U.S. Highway 101 north from Amanda Park to reach the Lake Quinault North Shore Road. Follow this road eastward; it is paved for the first 7 miles. Bear left at the junction at mile 12 and continue up the North Shore Rd. for the remaining 2.6 miles to the Irely Lake Trailhead, which is across the road from the North Fork Campground.

Key points:
0.0   Irely Lake Trailhead.
0.7   Trail crosses Irely Creek.
1.1   Spur path to Irely Lake.
1.3   Irely Lake.

The hike: The trail begins in the rainforest river bottoms of the Quinault's North Fork. It runs northward among the stout trunks of old-growth redcedar and Sitka spruce, climbing in short bursts across the forested benchlands. Ferns and mosses grow from every available surface, suffusing the landscape with green. After 0.7 mile the trail crosses tiny Irely

Creek and begins to follow its meandering, brush-choked channel. Salmonberries and thimbleberries grow side by side along the stream's course.

Soon a spur trail splits away to the left, running through a profusion of red huckleberries en route to the benches overlooking Irely Lake. (The berries ripen in August.) This

Irely Lake

large rainforest pool is surrounded by wet meadows, forming a rare and important pocket of wetland in the midst of the conifers. During the winter rainy season, the lake fills to the brim with water, but during the summer the water level drops as the lake water drains away through underground channels. Ospreys, waterfowl, and beaver are commonly seen at the lake and the surrounding marshes. During winter, herds of Roosevelt elk are sometimes spotted here. There is a primitive camping area at the north end, but mosquitoes are known to be fierce here. Retrace the trail from the lake to return to the trailhead.

24
SAMS RIVER LOOP

Type of hike: Loop.
Total distance: 2.8 miles.
Elevation change: Minimal.
Time required: 1.5 to 3 hours.
Maps: USGS Salmon River; Custom Correct *Queets Valley*.
Finding the trailhead: From the village of Queets, drive south-east 7 miles on U.S. Highway 101, then turn north on Queets Valley Road at mile 144.6. Follow this narrow gravel road (unsuited to trailers and RVs) for 13.8 miles to reach the trailhead at road's end.

Key points:

0.0   Queets River Trailhead. Hike east along the Sams River, a smaller tributary of the Queets.
0.3   Trail leaves Sam's River and turns inland.
1.5   Trail crosses Queets River Road near the Queets Ranger Station.
1.8   Trail reaches the banks of the Queets River.
2.7   Trail emerges on Queets River Road. Turn left on road to complete the loop.
2.8   Hike ends at Queets River Trailhead.

The hike: This short loop trail makes an easy circuit through the rainforest bottomlands of the Queets River. This remote corner of Olympic National Park receives few visitors

Sams River Loop

Queets River
Campground

To Spruce Bottom

Ford

Queets River

Queets River Road

Sam's River

Queets
Ranger
Station

N

0   .5   1

Miles

compared to the popular Hoh Rainforest area, and hikers are more likely to find solitude here.

The trail begins from the Queets River Trailhead, running eastward along the open banks of Sams River. The trail soon enters a rainforest of hemlock, Sitka spruce, and bigleaf maple that is underlain by a rich assortment of ferns and shrubs. The trail soon turns inland, passing a grove of red alder beside a small woodland brook. After crossing the brook, the trail enters a thicket of vine maples with moss-hung branches that form an archway over the trail. After some distance, this tunnel of greenery opens out into a large clearing, the former site of a homestead. A few feral fruit trees grow in the opening to mark the efforts of turn-of-the-century pioneers. Shrubs and ferns are encroaching as the forest slowly reclaims its own.

The trail passes through a stand of young spruce, then crosses Queets River Rd. to reach the ranger station. Nearing the Queets River, the trail crosses one more meadow and turns east along its sunny banks. Here, the massive boles of ancient spruces rise above a lush growth of sword ferns. The limpid, aquamarine waters of the Queets swirl lazily down a broad channel of gravel and sand. The trail emerges onto the road just below the camping area; turn left to follow the road back to the trailhead.

The Olympic Coastline

OVERVIEW

The wild and rugged Olympic coast is the site of ceaseless change. Wave action weathers arches and sea stacks from resistant blocks of sandstone, then slowly abrades them down to nothing. The fractured rock of the coves is constantly slumping onto the beach, then is carried away by the waves. Flood-gorged rivers discharge great plumes of silt and debris into the ocean, forming long spits at their mouths. Enormous logs are washed out to sea by these rivers; the logs are stripped and polished by the surf and then cast up on the beach. The incessant pounding of the waves, as well as the periodic tempests of wintertime, are constantly at work tearing down the coastline and building it anew.

This environment of endless upheaval is also the site of one of the most diverse biological communities in the Pacific Northwest. Tide pools harbor an almost infinite array of invertebrate life amid a lush growth of aquatic plants. Gulls, mergansers, ospreys, and bald eagles wheel on the ocean breezes, while oystercatchers and sandpipers patrol the beaches and rocks. The offshore islands teem with marine mammals, featuring sea otters, gray whales, orcas, harbor seals, and the endangered Steller's sea lion. Such a bounty of marine life formed the economic backbone of the coastal Indian villages, which have stood here from time immemorial.

Most of the coastline can be hiked, but a tide table is a

The Olympic Coastline

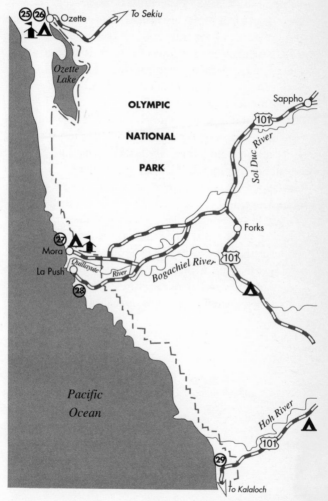

must because heavy surf renders most of the headlands impassable at high tide. Tide tables are posted at most trailheads, and free copies are usually offered as well. Avoid hiking on an incoming tide, and use common sense at all times. Changing weather patterns can result in higher tides than expected, especially when a storm is brewing. In addition, the surf often tosses huge (and deadly) logs around like match sticks, and in many cases these surf logs are waterlogged and invisible beneath the waves. Do not swim in the surf of unprotected beaches; venture into the water only in protected areas that have little wave action. NOTE: The water is extremely cold, even in summer.

Developed areas near the coast can be found at Lake Ozette, Mora, and Kalaloch. Kalaloch (pronounced "kuh-LAY-lock") has its own lodge, and campgrounds and ranger stations can be found at all of these locations. Lake Ozette is a popular (though remote) destination, and its small campground is often full. A private store called the Lost Resort has some supplies and extra campsites. Clallam Bay, Forks, and, to a lesser extent, Kalaloch offer groceries and other supplies.

25
CAPE ALAVA

Type of hike: Out-and-back.
Total distance: 6.6 miles roundtrip to Cape Alava; 8.6 miles round trip to the Wedding Rocks.
Elevation change: 200-foot gain, 240-foot loss to Cape Alava.
Time required: 4 to 8 hours, depending on speed and destination.
Maps: USGS Ozette; Custom Correct *Ozette Beach Loop*.
Finding the trailhead: From Sappho on U.S. Highway 101, drive north on Washington Highway 112 to Clallam Bay and the village of Sekiu. Turn left (south) 2.3 miles west of Sekiu on Hoko-Ozette Road, which is paved for its 20-mile length. The trailhead is located beside the ranger station at road's end.

Key points:
0.0   Ozette Ranger Station. Trail crosses Ozette River.
0.2   Trail splits into Sand Point and Cape Alava trails. Bear right.
3.3   Cape Alava. Turn south along the coast.
4.3   Wedding Rocks.

The hike: This trail offers a mid-range day hike to a part of the coast that is inaccessible by car. It receives heavy use due to its ease of access, and a permit reservation system is in place for overnight camping during summertime. Cape

Alava is known as a good spot for whale watching, and the mostly boardwalk trail passes a historic homestead site on the way to the coast. The only reliable fresh water along the route is at Cape Alava, and this is stained brown with tannins and should be treated. Wise hikers will bring along an abundant supply of water. Wear soft-soled shoes for traction on the boardwalk.

Cape Alava and Sand Point

The trail leaves the Ozette Ranger Station heading west, and a broad bridge soon arches above the sluggish waters of the Ozette River. Soon after entering the forest, the trail branches into two paths. The right fork heads toward Cape Alava and the left fork to Sand Point. Bear right on the Cape Alava Trail, which wanders west through young spruce and hemlock underlain by deer fern. The gigantic leaves of skunk cabbage appear in clumps in the boggy pockets of the forest.

The trail soon becomes a boardwalk causeway, which may be quite slippery (especially for hard-soled shoes) during rains. At mile 2.3 the trail passes a rest area that is actually the site of Lars Ahlstrom's barn, long since burned down. The broad stretch of coastal prairie to the west of it is named Ahlstrom's Prairie in honor of this man, who built the original causeway and was for a time the westernmost home-steader in the United States. A few fruit trees remain to the south of the trail, while the deteriorating buildings of the homestead lie out of sight to the north. This coastal prairie is really a wet bog, filled with sedges, crowberry, and sun-dews. The sundew is carnivorous: hairs on the leaves produce droplets of a sticky, sweet-smelling substance which traps ants and flies. After crossing this opening, the trail enters a superb coastal rainforest dominated by Sitka spruce and sword fern.

The trail then descends from the bluff to reach the shore-line at Cape Alava. Upon reaching the cape, visitors are immediately impressed by the collection of large, spruce-encrusted islands that loom offshore. To the north is Tskawayah Island, so close to shore that it can be reached on foot at low tide. This island is part of the Ozette Indian Reservation, and climbing onto it is not permitted. Far to the west, the Bodelteh Islands appear to be a single mass from this vantage point. The long, lean ridge of Ozette Island rises across a rocky tidal flat to the southeast.

Cape Alava is reputed to be one of the best places on the coast to see marine mammals, including the majestic gray whale. This whale is unusual in that it lives on a diet of amphipods that it filters from sea floor sediments. There are campsites among the trees and a tiny creek for fresh water; campers should be aware that racoons are particularly persistent pests in this area; keep packs and food out of reach.

The Makah Ranger Station lies a short distance to the north. A Makah village stood here for untold centuries, and a succession of mudslides buried the site from time to time. The slides resulted in one of the most important archaeological digs in North America. The dig site is currently inactive but should not be disturbed. A binder at the site contains a laminated magazine article that offers additional information on this historic village site, and artifacts are on display in the museum in Neah Bay. The last permanent residents of this village had departed by 1917, but the Makah still return to the small reservation just to the north on a seasonal basis.

Travelers who seek a longer trek can continue south along a trailless coastal route to reach the Wedding Rocks, a famous site of Makah petroglyphs. To reach the site, turn south, following a narrow strip of gravel that is deep and soft. A rocky shelf borders the beach, and at low tide the numerous tide pools provide windows into the world of sea creatures.

The first headland to be reached is the site of the Wedding Rocks, where a collection of 300-year-old petroglyphs grace the soft graywacke boulders. The petroglyphs are on boulders above the high-tide mark, clustered in two groups: one group is centered 50 yards to the north of the headland, while the other group is 25 yards southeast of it. There are more than 50 petroglyphs in all, featuring marine mammals, a two-masted sailing bark, and human figures. The most famous petroglyph is the "wedding scene" from which the rocks derive their name. It consists of a male and female figure surrounded by bisected circles, which are a sort of sexual symbol. Carving or defacing of the petroglyph site is a federal crime; please report any violations immediately. Turn around here to complete the hike.

26
SAND POINT

see map on page 92

Type of hike: Out-and-back.
Total distance: 6.2 miles (round trip).
Elevation change: 140-foot gain, 180-foot loss.
Time required: 3 to 5 hours.
Maps: USGS Ozette; Custom Correct *Ozette Beach Loop*.
Finding the trailhead: From Sappho on U.S. Highway 101, drive north on Washington Highway 112 to Clallam Bay and the village of Sekiu. Turn left (south) 2.3 miles west of Sekiu on Ozette Road, which is paved for most of its 20-mile length. The trailhead is located beside the ranger station at road's end.

Key points:
0.0   Ozette Ranger Station. Trail crosses Ozette River.
0.2   Trail splits into Sand Point and Cape Alava trails. Bear right.
3.0   Sand Point target. Follow trail east for Ozette Lake.
3.1   Sand Point.

The hike: This route leads from Ozette Lake to the coastline through an old burn in the coastal forest. This path is almost entirely boardwalk and has lots of stairs on it. At the end of the trail is Sand Point, with its sandy beaches strewn with driftwood. Keep an eye out for raccoons, which are particularly abundant around the Sand Point beaches; keep food safely out of reach.

The trail leaves the Ozette Ranger Station heading west, and a broad bridge soon arches above the sluggish waters of the Ozette River. Soon after entering the forest the trail branches into two paths. The right fork heads toward Cape Alava and the left fork to Sand Point. Turn left as the boardwalk leads into a shady coastal forest of Sitka spruce. The causeway soon breaks out into an old burn that is now a jungle of salal and other shrubs. A few old cedars survived the fire and rise high above the brushy understory. Just before reaching the coast, the boardwalk passes through a narrow band of timber to reach the sea.

The trail emerges at a target just south of Sand Point. True to its name, sandy beaches surround this long spit that juts into the Pacific. There are campsites among the trees to the south of the point, and the acidic waters of a tiny creek provide the only supply of water. Far out to sea the stately walls of White Rock rise sheer from the open ocean. Cormorants, common murres, and glaucous-winged gulls nest on this isolated stack, and their droppings give the island its white color. To complete the hike, follow the boardwalk back to the trailhead.

27
HOLE-IN-THE-WALL

Type of hike: Out-and-back.
Total distance: 3.2 miles (round trip).
Elevation change: Minimal.
Time required: 2 to 3.5 hours.
Maps: USGS La Push, Custom Correct *North Olympic Coast.*
Finding the trailhead: From Forks, drive about 1 mile north on U.S. Highway 101 to the La Push Road (Washington Highway 110). Turn left (west) and drive 7.6 miles to the fire station. Turn right here on the road to Mora, and continue 4.8 miles to the Rialto Beach Trailhead at road's end.

Keypoints:
0.0   Rialto Beach parking area. Turn north at the shoreline.
1.6   Hole-in-the-Wall. CAUTION: Do not attempt passing around the rock in more than a 5-foot tide.
2.3   Headland. CAUTION: impassable in a tide higher than 5 feet.

The hike: This trip visits a wild and beautiful stretch of coastline at the mouth of the Quillayute River. The coastline to the north is typified by boulder-strewn coves and rocky headlands, but this route covers only the sand and gravel strands of Rialto Beach. Easy access makes Rialto Beach a popular spot with tourists, particularly on weekends.

Hole-in-the-Wall

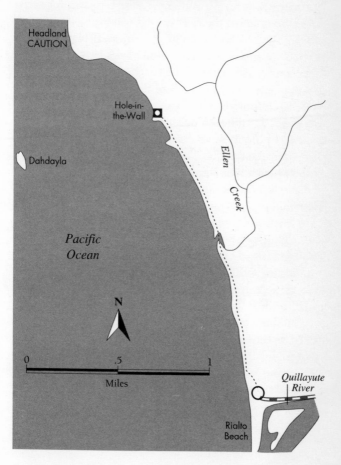

The trek begins at Rialto Beach, a cobble-strewn strand that extends north for 3 miles. Enormous drift logs have been carried down the river during winter floods, battered and polished by wave action, then heaved high onto the beach by storms. These same winter gales have sculpted the Sitka spruce, which crowd the beach in low-growing forms that resemble the krummholz of timberline. A long spit extends south from the mouth of the Quillayute River toward the James Island archipelago. This cluster of islands is guarded by stout, wave-carved cliffs of sandstone topped with spruce and alder. The Quileute tribe once used this cluster of islands as a natural fortress when fierce bands of Makah swept down the coast during the course of intertribal warfare.

As the route runs northward, Cake Rock is the major stack that rises far out to sea, while the more ragged crest of Dahdayla Island rises from the surf closer to the beach. The traveling is easy all the way to Hole-in-the-Wall Rock. True to its name, this minor promontory is pierced by a rounded aperture worn through the stone by centuries of wave action. A short trail climbs around the head, which can be passed on the ocean side only at low tides. Travelers seeking a longer hike can continue up the beach for another 0.7 mile before it becomes necessary to begin the hazardous headland crossings. Retrace your steps to complete the hike.

28
THE QUILLAYUTE NEEDLES

Type of hike: Out-and-back.
Total distance: 4.8 miles (round trip).
Elevation change: 120-foot gain, 200-foot loss.
Time required: 3 to 5 hours.
Maps: USGS La Push and Quillayute Prairie; Custom Correct *South Olympic Coast*.
Finding the trailhead: From Forks, drive north about 1 mile on U.S. Highway 101 to La Push Road (Washington Highway 110). Turn left (west) and drive 12.7 miles (following signs for La Push) to the well-marked Second Beach Trailhead.

Keypoints:
0.0   Second Beach Trailhead.
0.7   Trail reaches the beach. Turn south.
2.1   Headland. CAUTION: 4-foot tide.
2.2   Headland. CAUTION: 1-foot tide.
2.4   Teahwhit Head. DANGER: impassable headland.

The hike: This route follows the Second Beach Trail down to a sandy stretch of coastline, offering a day hike or a short overnight trip. This area is known for its diverse tide-pool life. (Feel free to observe, but don't disturb it.) If you plan to travel around any of the headlands here, carry a current tide table and make sure that the critical water level stays lower than the levels noted above when attempting a passage.

The trail begins by winding through a forest of Sitka spruce and western hemlock that sprang up in the aftermath of logging that occurred early in this century. After wandering the wooded blufftop for a time, a wooden boardwalk and steps drop down to the north end of Second Beach. An enormous block of contorted stone named Quateata

The Quillayute Needles

blocks the northern approaches to the beach, and it is pierced by a natural arch. The Quillayute Needles are scattered across the sparkling waters of the Pacific. This formation is an old wave-cut terrace that has been elevated and weathered into sandstone pillars. Some are massive and stout while others form slender spires.

Turn south and follow the coast as it bends away toward Teahwhit Head. The beach spreads out into a wide stretch of fine sand, raked ceaselessly by turbulent combers. Near its south end sheer cliffs march down to the water's edge, and tortured stacks stand among the breakers. Tide pools among the rocks showcase delicate sea anemones and colorful sea stars. A passage can be made around the first headland, which guards an isolated beach. From this point a natural arch can be seen among the jagged spires of Teahwhit Head. The next headland is trickier to negotiate and can only be crossed during extremely low tides. Beyond it is a secluded cove much like the previous inlet, and a rugged jumble of boulders stretches southwest toward the forbidding and impassable cliffs of Teahwhit Head. Turn around to complete the hike.

29
RUBY BEACH

Type of hike: Out-and-back.
Total distance: 0.8 mile to mouth of Cedar Creek.
Elevation change: 180-foot loss.
Time required: 30 to 60 minutes.
Maps: USGS Destruction Island; Custom Correct *South Olympic Coast*.
Finding the trailhead: From Kalaloch, drive north on U.S. Highway 101 to the Ruby Beach parking area at mile 164.7.

The hike: This route leads down to one of the beaches that stretch along the southern coast of the Olympic Peninsula, a broad and almost unbroken strand that stretches between the Hoh and Queets rivers. A trail leads down to the beach, at which point day trips of any length can be undertaken. Camping on these beaches is not allowed. Pets, however, are permitted here.

Ruby Beach is known for its pinkish sands, which derive their color from the presence of tiny grains of garnet. Ruby is set apart from the other beaches in the Kalaloch area by the presence of sea stacks at its northern end; Abbey Island is the largest of these. Cedar Creek forms a wide and brackish lagoon near the stacks, and piles of drift logs litter its edges. Destruction Island can be seen far to the southwest. This mighty rock has lived up to its name over the years, being the site of at least five major shipwrecks. Follow the route back to the parking area to complete the hike.